# WE OVER HERE NOW

We Over Here Now
Published through Brick Cave Media

Interior Book Design and Layout by
www.integrativeink.com

ISBN-10: 1938190114
ISBN-13: 978-1-938190-11-7

Cover art: "Shipwrecked" © Mark Higgins

Thanks to the editors of the following publications in which these poems first appeared:

"To the High School Thug That Broke into His English Teacher's Car" first appeared in *Rattle*.

"Comfort Woman's Gold" first appeared in *World Literature Today*.

"I Hate Zombies like You Hate Me" first appeared in *Pank*.

"Allegedly" first appeared in *The New Verse News*.

brickcavebooks.com

# WE OVER HERE NOW

Poems by Scott Woods

# CONTENTS

# PART I.

## WHAT THE BLACK POETS WILL
## KILL ME FOR TELLING YOU

Never mind the trees and the wind sitting in their lines,
their limbs folded pleasant, broken clean in their laps:
all of their poems are black.

They don't want to shake those bones every time you ask.
They want to write poems about their obsession
with BBC shows without having to point out
why there can never be a black Doctor Who.

All of the rhythm ascribed to their poetry
in their introductions doesn't hit on the one.
They need a jazz poem as bad as you do, more.

Despite their odes to the chain link gods,
none of them can actually play basketball.
There isn't one of them who wouldn't trade their tenure

for a championship ring.
You should see them at the meetings.
So much cream and sugar in their Styrofoam cups

you'd think the coffee foreplay.
They leave the magazine with their picture on the cover
in the seat next to you by accident.

Do not be fooled by the Hottentots
or the smell of vinyl revolutions
or the streetlight cool brownstone steps they all use

to braid someone's hair on.
These are the bones required for admission,
the voodoo they beg to be cursed by,
the blue notes firing around the campfire
like drunken cigarette butts tossed into an inkwell.

## WHUPPIN'S

A whuppin' is a ritual.

I agree: a smack on the back of the head
is degrading, borders on abuse.
But a whuppin'?
A whuppin' is an understanding.

Praying to leather belt gods,
extension cord deities,
flying shoes made missiles,
switches ripped from the arms of
understanding trees.

Some of you
will not understand
what I am talking about.
Some of you
will nod your heads and
feel the breath of a ghost belt
whispering in your ears.

My mother was an educated woman
but she couldn't count to save her life.
Ten whuppin's were frequently thirteen.
She blamed my squirming.
I blamed her Nelsonville education.

Vision borne from whuppin' #233:
I have seen the skillet swing of a
short woman who doesn't care what you think
reaching for a son too tall for bending
over bedsides anymore.
Goliath slain by cast iron love.

And the difference between a
whuppin' and abuse is
knowing when the lesson is over, and knowing
that in the swing there is love,
and in your calls for her
death between snivels,
you always knew the truth:
you deserved it.
You may not have deserved thirteen,
but ten was your magic number.

I have seen the generation
that will not understand this poem,
that will see a victim in its author.
You have not been spared.
Your scars will come to you and one day
you will look into a mirror
marvel at how much even
smooth skin can hide.
Every scar is not a welt that will not go away.
You will cut scars into your face
with laughter you do not mean
to hide pain you cannot share.

But I?
I can talk to my mother.
I know her reach.
It is deeper than skin or
the depth of a leather belt.

It is the distance between two hearts
that know what the other is capable of,
which is to say,
it is no distance at all.

## TO THE HIGH SCHOOL THUG WHO BROKE INTO HIS ENGLISH TEACHER'S CAR

What you know about Nina Simone
could do laps on a pencil tip,
so I'm struggling to understand
why you would steal that CD.

That you skipped the vodka in the glove compartment
but took my reading glasses is equally perplexing.

It's not my fault you can't handle grammar,
but it may be my fault it never took.
Allow me the honor of tutelage now:
Name the verb in the following sentence:

*Nina Simone sings.*

Not knowing what kind of grades you get in math,
let me point out that you have a 50/50 shot here.

What will you make of the ugly woman
who sings so sweetly from the bottom of her stories
that she becomes beautiful?
That you long for her entreating loneliness in the night
and wonder why girls today can't do it like that anymore?

How will you explain the mourning tripping out
of your poster-covered bedroom and into
the hallway, making your momma wonder
who got into her momma's records?

Nina Simone knows who you are and why you took that,
why the record called to you when fear struck your senses.

Nina Simone sings and I know you don't understand yet
the ramifications of what you've done,
how getting kicked out of your English class doesn't make it okay.

I know you couldn't possibly have conceived
that there are people in this world
who can show you their love in three notes.

You had no idea that some people need songs like that,
songs that reach through time and pull your heart down like
fire alarms and run through the hallways of your soul,
banging on the doors,
trying to get the demons to walk out civilly,
in a straight line just outside your mouth,
falling into a vodka double-shot you can't lift on your own.

I want to imagine you just like that:
sitting in your bedroom,
staring out a window cracked from your previous
shenanigans,
headphones to your skull,
scanning liner notes in my reading glasses,
Nina Simone singing long and hard into the night,
after a moment of trifling anger,
to see a beautiful thing and imagine it could save your life,
sometimes,
like it does mine,
every time the moon hangs there like it's harvest time,
pregnant with mankind's wishes,
heavy with the sorrow of thieves.

## THE ORGANIST

I have two suits:
one for when I meet with families,
one for when I play.

I got ten ties to make it look like I got ten suits.
Three black ties, two gold ties, one white tie,
two red, two blue,
depending on the affiliation of the deceased.

I have had three guns aimed at me
for playing something I had no business playing.

How many times have I pounded out Boyz II Men and
"Amazing Grace" for people who either
don't know the words or didn't know they child?

They families dance to what I play
like the church is a Saturday night hole-in-the-wall
and they song just came on.
They dance to whatever part of them
remembers the rhythm of death,
that hears a tambourine in its rattling conclusion
instead of gunshots and truth.

How many times have I played
until the only person left in the room
was me, the body, and the undertaker
giving me the cutthroat sign
the minute the sanctuary emptied out?
How many times was it just me and a body,
stuffed into a new suit that's gonna' cost
somebody rent that month, the organ standing in
for God's voice saying hello and goodbye at once?

I don't want no music when I die.
I know what musicians think,
shoved into the back of the show between gigs that day,
counting the minutes like ashtray gas money.
It's just a gig to us.
If it were someone we cared about in the box
we wouldn't be able to press the keys
on that organ to begin with.

# HOW TO MAKE A CRACKHEAD

In high school, lead her on.
Let her write you notes in class,
beautiful professions of love beyond her years.

Never respond.
Let her buy you lunch.
Never reciprocate.

Knock her milk over.
Never sit with her.
Never act like you know her.

Make her the ugly one,
the one it's okay to laugh at on buses.
Laugh at her.

Start the joke that makes others
laugh at her.

Smack her neck in class.
Then, when no one is looking,
kiss her.

Let her take you in her arms,
her tongue full and moving for you.
Kiss her back. Kiss her like love fills you up at her touch.

Make the footnote in her love letters come alive.
Kiss her with your eyes open to see if anyone can see you.
Let her see you with your eyes open.

Apologize, tell her you'll make it up to her.
Take her to the locker room.
Make love.

Take her to the auditorium.
Make love.

Take her to a hooptie in the parking lot.
Make love.

Give her things to write about in her diary for weeks, a year.
Let her find herself in you.
Show her how to make love.

Enjoy.

Then smack her neck in class again.
Disown her.
Pretend it never happened.

Strangle the words out of her like a drunk's last drop.
Ignore her when anyone else is around,
love her where no one will know.

Graduate.
Fuck her.
Move on.

Forget her number.
Forget her middle name.
Forget the smell of jheri curls in a locker room.

Grow up.
Be a man, grow up.
Be a man, learn love, then lose it.

Cry like men cry.
Love like men love.
Grow cool and Super Bowl-esque and modern.

See her on the street and remember.
See her on the street walking too fast on too-small legs,
shorts too short for fall.

Remember.
Feel guilty.
Remember.

See her look at you outside a carry-out,
a smile with memories for teeth.
Hug her quick anyway.

Let jheri curls fill your neck.
Remember.
Remember the woman you killed
when you strangled the girl with your tongue.

## WHEN YOUR WHITE FRIEND SAYS "NIGGER" BY ACCIDENT

Whatever you are doing must stop.
No one can speak for three seconds.
You must look him in the eye.
If you were not looking at your white friend
when he said the word, you must then turn your head
thusly, then look him in the eye.
You cannot smile, chuckle or snort.

You must calculate any debts
your relationship may have incurred.
You must take stock of any video games
that may have been left at his place.
You must recall instantly who drove.
You must consider if you will now reveal
whether or not you slept with his sister.
You must do all of these things
in the time it takes you to make said eye contact.

Then you must consider if this is truly your friend.
You must consider if you have made him comfortable
in this bed you are about to ask him to lie in.
You must consider if you have been any kind of friend at all.

And then, you must consider
if you have been a nigger.

## GHETTO CONGRESS

Clothes lines snapping sunlight from their dresses
Flags bearing twenty-second floored nations
Citizens milling the ghetto valleys
Lobbying brown bottle bag amendments
Sidewalk legislators debate crap rolls
Gin senators take the floor of nightclubs
Pleading jukebox law, demanding barroom rights
Billiard constitutions signed in smoke rings

# HOW TO BUILD A JUKE JOINT

Start with something that
wasn't never meant to be social:
a convenience store, a shotgun shack, a garage.
A garage is a fine start-up.

Wear it down.

Invite a friend over for a beer while you
workin' on their car,
every beer another point shaved off
what you may ask for someday.
Put a radio in the back, behind the
toolbox, to make the time pass just-so.
Stop pissing in the corners and
take it out back.
Invite that friend back over.
Tell him, bring his friends,
with change to spare.

Move the oil rags from the orange crates.
Move the orange crates to make room for folding chairs.
Move the car guts and steel jacks.
Move the oil bucket to make room for a cooler.
Move in an electrical wire spool and make table of it.

Run 2x4s and cover them in
whatever boards come to you.
Sheet metal will suffice, but
not above the Mason-Dixon line.

Remove the old light bulb and run
Christmas lights out its socket
until the ceiling disappears in
shadow or summer yuletide.

Set your rituals.
Don't bother with framing that first dollar;
you'll be spending it.
Make everyone tip their hats to the
Martin Luther King picture instead.

Never hire anybody;
everyone earns they keep the
old-fashioned way: ale equity.
A bartender who stands at it
when he's working and
sits at it when he's not
is ideal.

Know your regulars.
Advertise liquor you don't have to instill hope.
Occasionally serve easy meats and whispering pies.
Call drunkards by their traits,
only by their momma's names when
they can't come back no more.
Let the fast girls rub the slow men to sleep.
Let their pearls hit the dusty worn
cuffs of the farmer.
Let the deacon have the booth in the back.

Borrow the church piano and
never give it back.
Draw a line at the blues.
Let the nightclubs play music;
this a juke joint.
Give the band about three feet of space to work.
Make the guitar player sit in the audience
and the singer stand behind the bar.
They all want to anyway.
Call it Blue Monday even when it's Thursday,
but never call a Friday anything but payday.

Paint your dirty fingernails in class:
throw down a rug under the card table
you reserve for special guests.
Nail up curtains where there ain't no windows.
Have no dress code save the cutting eyes
of those who don't appreciate
things too new in the
vicinity of their shrines.
Keep it respectable.
(Respectable meaning, your sweatpants
can't have no holes in them.)

Put in a fan even if it will not
divorce the wet shirts from
their masters.

If the roof leaks, leave it.
You need the holes and cracks to let
the Swamp Folk come and go
as they please.
If Mother Nature sees fit to knock a
good-sized hole in said roof that
bypasses quaint,
every table then becomes negotiable.

Set up a lost & found in case
someone needs a hairpin or
the band needs a harp in B-flat or you
need a spare .25 bullet.
Keep your pens in a cigar box
and your cigars in your pocket.

Never put in anything new.
View decoration as either a
personal vendetta or a communal effort.

Make it the pimp's living room,
the wino's heaven.
Let the tramps stamp it with their spit and
their knife-carved memories,
right into the bar.

Above all, own it.  Never share it.
Brand it with your fists.
Tongue its tiles and pool stick-poked panels.
Swim in its flooded stalls.
Sleep in its booths and to the jukebox's
skipping 45s.

Keep makin' a job of it,
every night.
Never make it home.
That's everyone else's job.
Your job is to keep the drinks cold and
handy, and to make sure that
when the bulldozers come,
you don't have a tear left to shed.

## EVERYTHING YOU NEED TO KNOW ABOUT PRINCE IN 13 SONGS

### 1. When Doves Cry
The lack of a bass line is symbolic.
It represents the failing of the nuclear family,
the feeling one navigates when one's
support system has been de-functionalized.

The solo guitar at the beginning?
The one that screams and grinds and finally chokes?
That's symbolic, too.
It's representative of me forcing a tour bus to
turn around, drive through our old neighborhood
until I find your old car, and key it with a guitar pick
I got from B. B. King.

As far as doves go, I just think they're pretty.

### 2. Adore
Much ado has been made about what sex with me must be like.
It is, of course, all true.
I come from a long line of lovers who adulterated reality,
who closed bedroom doors with our dicks and
transformed living rooms into moonscapes
or the steps of Versailles or galleries of framed ecstasies frozen
in time.
Across the room, I see you biting your lip.
You are wondering what I will do to you,
if there really are 23 positions in a one night stand.
And then it hits you: oh my god, you think,
he is making me come without touching.
And you are right.
That is what number 17 feels like.

But it has been so long since I have slept
in my own bed.
I consume hotels and apartments for months,
only to come home to perform again
for the cook and the gardener and maids.
The scenery rolls away from behind me but the play goes on.
Every breath I take is theater in the round.

An interviewer once joked if I had any idea
how many babies were made to my music.
"1,732,311," I said.
Then we just waited for the other to blink.

### 3. Lady Cab Driver
She was beautiful like a ghetto is beautiful,
missing her front teeth and singing my songs before
she even knew I was back there.
I was prone to disguises then.
Back then, the world didn't quite bend to my will
every time I entered a room.
I asked her what she thought of him.
She said she loved Prince,
that a Friday night just wasn't a Friday night
if she couldn't play him.
She drove too fast,
honked her horn in time with the music instead of traffic,
and dropped me off in a haze of exhaust and frankincense
billowing out of a stick of incense jammed into her
air conditioner vent.
I wrote this song for her that night.
It wasn't supposed to be sexual.
She was an angel—an angel with a smile like a cage,
or a target, depending on who was kissing her.
When I kissed her on my way out of the cab
in my mind, they were pearly gates.

## 4. Little Red Corvette
I keep my hair long because it still smells like her
and that's how I want her:
in my eyes,
catching at the edge of my mouth when I sing her gospel,
sweating out into my cheeks in Super Bowl rain.

She laughed like a ribcage of firecrackers,
held her belly when she laughed.
her hair bounced even when she didn't move,
unseen tremors in her, shaking her at the shoulders,
hugging her from behind.
Fat-fingered, like she made sailor knots out of telephone poles,
but when she dug past my waves to the scalp
I forgot my name.

Every time I called her she answered with, "What you want?"
She said when I spoke to her
she could hear which words I replaced
with numbers and Wingdings,
that even "goodbye" was a fable.
She bought me a pair of sneakers for my birthday
even when she knew no one would ever see me in them.
I bought her a car.
Sometimes, when I'm home and walking the streets,
I see it.
She's really let it go.
Which is to say, she's really let me go, too.

## 5. Condition of the Heart
She said she wished I played piano more often.
I told her that wasn't how the child wanted to be born that day.
She begged me to stop speaking in piano stool cranks.
I told her the tongue chooses the man.

I'm actually most proficient on the piano.
I just let them think it's the guitar because
nobody danced while playing a piano better
than Jerry Lee Lewis.  And if a white boy's going to

beat you at your own music, play something else.
I know a part of you is screaming out Elvis or Keith Richards,
to which the Bible responds in Psalm 95:1 with, and I quote:
"Jimi Hendrix."

"Owuwah."
When I spell "owuwah," I spell it o-w-u-w-a-h.
It doesn't mean anything you can put words to,
and that's why no one's ever spelled it the same way twice.
It's what I say to all of my weaknesses,
a bleating of pain, ecstasy and questioning.
I used to keep track of the real ones,
the ones who loved me back.
But after the ecstasy was pain, and after the pain was
the question, "Why am I never enough for you?"

## 6. The Beautiful Ones
It doesn't take a rich or beautiful man to steal fire from gods.
I have been left for simple men many times:
Two school teachers, an insurance salesman, a roadie,
a painter who'd only sold one painting his entire life.
None of them prettier than me.
None of them rich.
None of them able to do the splits.
Sometimes all you have to do is be there,
rake a pile of leaves, make snowballs with their kids.
I haven't done yard work since I was eighteen years old,
and snow doesn't get to touch my skin anymore, I'm so handled.
I haven't felt snow on my face in thirty years.
I haven't felt snow.
And it seems like I haven't felt her
in about the same.

## 7. Joy In Repetition
I sometimes wonder how long I'll write these songs for you.
I still write them because you kiss the moon's wrists when you
whisper in your sleep.
I scratch lyrics out of you where pillows warm in the shadow
of your lips.

I sometimes wonder how long I'll write these whispers for you.
I still kiss them because you scratch the moon's lips when you
sleep in your whisper.
I sing lyrics out of your shadows warm in the pillows of your
lips.

I sometimes wonder how long I'll whisper these pillows for you.
I still scratch them because you moon the wrist's lips when
you shadow your kiss.
I warm pillows out of you where scratches warm in the lips of
your shadow.

I sometimes kiss how long I'll whisper these wrists for you.
I still write moons because you wonder the lips.
I pillow warmth out of your scratches where shadows sleep in
you.

## 8. Let's Go Crazy
Dearly beloved,
you have been ejected from the band because
you refused to wear black face.
That, and you missed a gig because of a freak
snowstorm in Atlanta.
That, and you play drums better than I do.
We both know that it is not enough for people to think
I can play 20 instruments.
They must believe I can play them better than you.
If they had any idea how bad I am on saxophone
I'd have to turn in half my boot collection.

Dearly beloved,
you have been ejected from the band because
I require a new sound curiously like an old sound
we have forgotten.
That, and I could use another light-skinned dude
to break up all this funk.
That, and it isn't unheard of for Andre Cymone
to keep finding my numbers and call,
and I meet him somewhere uptown,

which is really just downtown when it's laughing at the pigeons,
and we borrow axes from the resident lumberjacks
and chop down the beanstalks of fame and anonymity,
sit together on the edge of the hoofer's stage,
switching from lead to rhythm to heartbeats to
beating on cardboard boxes with plastic
spoons and chicken bones, still dreaming about
how it was gonna be, and what it never was, and still trying
to figure out why we still had holes in our chests,
like searching for absolutes in rain water,
spilling from our throats, our strings, our fingers.

Dearly beloved,
you have been ejected from the band because
no one can play for me and do drugs.
That, and I found you leafing through my records
at the last house party.
That, and I can tell from the way you play
you'd rather be Buddy Miles than Mitch Mitchell.

## 9. Old Friends 4 Sale
It's not because they don't honor the contracts.
That's not why I sued them.
I have signed so many contracts.
Contracts are just paper.
Contracts are a con.  It's why we call them that.
You don't really have to honor a contract.
So that's not why I sued them.
I sued them because they broke my heart.
The singer with a tongue like a cat,
the guitarist who should have known better,
the cook I spent thousands of dollars a week on,
only to have to make macaroni and cheese every night.
All heartbreakers, all suddenly able to find lawyers.
All brothers and sisters I wanted to show heaven
if only they would honor my name.

## 10. Darling Nikki

Her name wasn't Nicole,
it wasn't a hotel lobby and there was a magazine,
but she didn't need it.
When she tells me now that she's seeing someone
that doesn't belong to her, I realize I've failed.
The way I made her feel was supposed to change this.
I don't mean naked; I mean the music was supposed to do this.

You were so mad that night.
The sun was so serious it refused to set
so we walked under a crimson bodyguard of afternoon,
an apocalypse dusk, a cherry moon,
every pink cloud a question or an elegy.
You didn't want to be a secret anymore,
and I only speak in whispers except when I'm praying.

You were always so good at naming things.
You named us a covenant of parades,
called all of my funny faces interviews of hunger,
drowned my every attempt to solo instead of argue.
I've fired girlfriends for less, but kept them for worse.
I flew you around the world,
fed you starfish soup aged in the violet and peach-rimmed
cups of octopus limbs,
the French Riviera bent at its waist to drop
diamonds into the lockets on your ankles.
I had no idea you had no intention of staying,
and the religion you gave me,
wherein heaven lies in your face to be had after
slogging through our hell storms,
that was gone,
Olympus snuffing out its creation,
or its creation snuffing out its gods.

I just wanted to talk to you sometime.

It didn't always have to be pillows and Nag Champa
and Doritos breath.

I made the end of your song play backwards.
I wanted to talk to you without all the work,
but then I wanted you to feel like you had to earn it.
You just decided it was easier to lift the needle
before the end of the record and never write anymore.
Now I listen to everything backwards.
Oh, I give it a chance at first, but inevitably I end up
putting a hand to the platter and pulling the words
back into me.

## 11. Housequake
The boogie man in my closet wasn't scary at all.
He looked like James Brown,
kicking open the door off its hinges,
kneeling to pray to the funk behind him,
then sliding to the side, yanking floorboards out of their
grooves like a tidal wave,
then twisting in place so hard and fast
the carpet churned up onto his ankles, his shins, his waist,
then hung there like a shaggy kilt on a
sweating, panting Scotsman with a smile
that could put a hole in the sun's eyes.

When my mother stormed in
and whupped us for staying up late
and tearing up our bedroom,
it was a beating I took gladly.
Her leaving the record on in the living room that night
while she lay on a couch with a man I never met,
playing "Hot Pants" on a console stereo as big as a coffin,
I had found my purpose.
And if it meant a few midnight beatings after a visit
from the ghost of funk's future,
it was a small price to pay.

## 12. Sometimes It Snows In April
*Q: What has 18 balls and 3 pubic hairs?*
*A: A Michael Jackson slumber party.*

24

I fired the technician who told that joke backstage
before a show in Paris, right on the spot.
Stormed right out of my dressing room with one boot on.
Then the story became Prince breaking a boot off in a guy's
ass in France once.

Our thing was never about who was better.
We both know who played what and who did not.
It's right there in the music,
one side of the platter the confessions of a saint,
the other always finding reasons to end up in
confessionals at the end of tours.
No one ever said they hated you to your face.
Don't let John Lennon fool you:
fame is still very much like wearing a bulletproof vest.
But if you ever touch the ground, ever become like a man,
they will slay you.
That you named a son after me
always meant the world to me.
Michael, when I dance I am praying for you.

## 13. Purple Rain

Contrary to public opinion, this is the first song I ever wrote.
I know it sounds good later, but we should be honest now.
You and I both knew this was how it was going to be:
strings and applause and Alicia Keys stealing shit.

You'd think the guitar would break at its neck
when I touch it because I'm so pretty, but it doesn't.
It says, *You're not that pretty.*
It says, *You're not the first Napoleon I've stranded on an island.*
It says, *You don't work my strings; I work yours.*
  *And while you are pretty enough,*
  *let's not confuse which of us*
  *is the marionette.*
  *It's probably best that you break it up*
  *with some dancing now and then.*
  *At least then you are free.*

If you're not in love you can still write about it.
If the music still won't come, then write about stalking.
Half of my slow jams are odes to stalking beautiful women
that don't really like short brothers
no matter how high their heels are;
that don't even know I'm in the room,
even when they're looking at me,
even when they cry out my name
and beg me to sign their breasts.

I don't dance this way because I can't control my limbs
or because I don't know what I'm going to do next.
I need you to think that if you get too close you might get hurt,
because you might, and I have the records to prove it.
I have been known to destroy a woman with love,
to immortalize her in such a way that she can never die,
and that if she does she will be known as having been mine
before any other thing she might have done in her life gets a shot.
The dash between the dates on their tombstones filled
with me and my words, and my touch, and my solos, and my hair
and never, in a million years,
will the reverse ever be true.
My hyphen will be filled with songs
and dancing and parties and hair,
not who I loved or who I lay or who found
parts of me worth saving for the next go-round.

I hope that our religion is true,
that there is a place in this world made of
your skin and your hands that speaks our names openly.
For if there is not, then there is no point,
and half of these songs could have been written by anybody.

## BLACK BARBERSHOP PRICE LIST

Men's Haircuts - $13
Beard Trim - $7
Razor Shaves - $12
Edge-up - $6
Edge-up with razor - $7
Parts - $3 and up
Kids Haircuts - $11
Disorderly Children - $5 extra per bad-ass child
Political Conversation - $4
Political Conversation that slights Obama - $20
Lowdown on who got locked up - $3
Lowdown on who got shot - $10
Lowdown on Down Low - $7
Lowdown on who got weed - $5 and a cut
2Pac is alive - $5
2Pac was in here last week - $8
World Affairs - $4
Michael Jackson didn't do nothin' to them kids - $6
"Martin Luther the King" scene from "Coming to America" - $10
Afros - $15
Eyebrow Arch - $5
Facials - $9
Church - Free

## ALLEGEDLY

*In eight chilling recordings, made the night of February 26, listeners can hear the frightened voices of neighbors calling to report screams for help, gunfire and then that someone was dead.*

—*Huffington Post* 3/16/2012 regarding the
alleged shooting by a block watch captain of
seventeen-year-old Trayvon Martin.

"Allegedly killed" must mean
someone is allegedly dead.
I didn't see the body, so I guess that's possible,
except there is a woman on television
who swears up and down
her son was shot.
Not allegedly. Shot for real.
And dead. Quite dead, for real.
Of course, she wasn't there either.
All she saw was a body.
We assume.

Perhaps we *assume* he was killed,
*assume* the worst, like we desire to jump
to these conclusions. To what end?
To move on? To get to the forgetting part?
Allegedly, someone stopped living.
Ergo, what? Nothing is true until someone says it is.
Body can't speak for itself.
Body's just a guess.
You weren't there.
Bullets don't mean anything.
The only thing that matters
is the truth you can prove.

We can prove dead.
We can prove bullet.
We can prove child.

We can prove pocket full of Skittles,
a hand full of iced tea.
We can prove pleading for one's life,
but not that life. That life is alleged.
Have yet to verify that life.
Could have been anyone passing through,
pleading for their lives on a Sunday night.
You can't prove that.
We can prove only
dead.
Only bullet.
Only child and Skittles and sweet tea.
That is the truth you can prove.

The truth is: I don't even look at the pictures anymore.
Already seen that album, know there will be
a dozen pictures of him ten years old,
smiling, not at all like the kids I see everyday
who hate everything, wear disinterest like
school uniforms. Family don't got none of those.

One picture will be a Halloween costume.
One will be so young you won't even recognize
the alleged victim, just the wood paneling
in the living room that is, yes, that old.
One, two little league football pictures.
A picture of him washed in a kitchen sink.
If there is enough alleged mystery here,
enough traction for our attention,
there will be a picture of him
that doesn't look like a black boy at all:
smiling, holding a stack of books,
his arm around a white friend no one
remembers anymore.
Lots of baby pictures. Elementary graduations.

Never sweat pants.
Never jogging suits.
Never that sneer that allegedly says nothing is worthy.

That's not a sneer, his father corrects.
That's just a bad angle.
His son never looked like that. His son
only knows brotherhood, candy vice,
only knows the backyard way to a convenience store,
knows now the plugging of a hairless chest
with a steel fingertip.
But then, his father wasn't there either
even though everything in him
cried out to make it so.

We must assume.

We can prove scream.
We can prove cry for help.
We can prove gunshot.
We can prove silence.
What we cannot prove
never happened

allegedly.

# PART II.

# THE BIBLE IN 50 HAIKU

## *The Old Testament*

1) Creation
   In the beginning
   The Lord said, "Let there be light."
   Monday mornings born.

2) The Garden of Eden
   All manner of beasts.
   A perfect world...until God
   decides to make Man.

3) Adam
   You don't need a leaf
   when you're the only person
   in the whole wide world.

4) Eve
   Lord, I'd like a friend.
   "I can help you for a cost."
   How much is one rib?

5) The Tree of Life & The Serpent
   It hisses to her,
   says this apple will make the
   smartest applesauce.

6) Cain & Abel
   Showing his brother
   how to pray properly was
   Abel's sacrifice.

7) Noah's Ark
   The Lord asked Noah,
   "Do you have any questions?"
   What is a cubit?

8) The Flood
The Ark is smelling.
It has been raining for days.
No toilet paper.

9) The Tower of Babel
Trying to reach God,
tongues struck senseless, no meaning.
Politicians born.

10) Lot Flees
As the cities burn
Lot's wife turns to see the flames.
Sodium woman.

11) Abraham Prepares to sacrifice Isaac
"Pop quiz, Abraham:
Just how much do you love me?"
He sharpens his knife.

12) Jacob Wrestles the Angel
Atomic elbow
Feathers held down on canvas.
Jacob on the ropes.

13) Joseph and The Coat of Many Colors
His brothers didn't know:
In time, a coat like that
will just be bad plaid.

14) Baby Moses
Thank God for rivers:
no diapers in the basket.
Wet outside and in.

15) The Burning Bush
No one else would claim
bushes spoke to them until
Rastafarians.

16) Moses: Staff to Snake
Pharaoh squirmed and said,
"Neat trick, Moses, but still I
will not let them go."

17) The Ten Plagues
Blood, frogs, gnats, swarms, boils,
disease, hail, locusts, darkness.
Babies hurt the most.

18) Releasing the Hebrew Slaves
Pharaoh changed his mind.
What good has ever come out
of the embattled?

19) The Parting of the Red Sea
Moses parts the sea.
Someone has the nerve to
complain about the mud.

20) The Ten Commandments
Thou shalt not kill.
(...unless thou art American,
white, or very rich.)

21) Joshua and Jericho
Cursed be the man
before God that riseth up
and rebuilds this place.

22) Idol worship
Even the smallest
coincidence can make us
believe in false gods.

23) Samson and Delilah
Strongest man ever
felled by a woman's touch and
a pair of scissors.

24) David and Goliath
   A shepherd boy kills
   a giant with a slingshot,
   a rock, and his faith.

25) King David
   When he hears of
   Saul's death, he looks to his hands and
   wishes they were stones.

26) Solomon
   Wisdom is easy:
   Just pull out a knife until
   One of them owns up.

27) Elijah on the chariot
   Set fire to wet wood.
   Ascended to Heaven.
   A gangster prophet.

28) Jezebel
   Power gone to her
   head. Jehu says she's really
   gone to the dogs.

29) Daniel and the Lions
   Daniel, lions, den.
   Frightening, though it turns out
   they don't like dark meat.

30) Jonah and the Whale
   Three days and nights spent
   in the belly of a whale?
   Sounds fishy to me.

31) Job
   Satan removed his
   wealth, his health and his family,
   yet he still believed.

36

32) Mary and Joseph
   A tough conversation
   to have with your husband,
   no matter his faith.

33) Jesus is born
   The Messiah is born!
   But no one in the stable
   dares spank his bottom.

34) Three Wise Men
   They ride many miles,
   stopping only to pick up
   frankincense and myrrh.

35) John the Baptist
   His head on its side,
   eyes open on a platter.
   Mouth wide, still preaching.

36) Jesus Miracle: Water to Wine
   It's not a party
   until Jesus shows up,
   turns water into wine.

37) Jesus Miracle: Heal the Crippled
   Raise the sickly man
   through a hole in the roof.
   Jesus will see him now.

38) Jesus Miracle: Loaves and Fishes
   Five thousand people
   listened to sermons all day.
   Gonna need more fish.

39) Jesus Parable: The Good Samaritan
The priest and the Levite
pass you by, but I?
I will tend to your wounds.

40) Jesus Parable: The Prodigal Son
Son, thou art ever
with me, and all that I have
is thine.  Lost, then found.

41) Jesus Miracle: Exorcises demons into pigs
"We are Legion!"
Jesus casts them out and says,
"Now? You are bacon."

42) Jesus Miracle: Walks on Water
The Apostles feared
the storm while at sea. So Jesus
met them halfway.

43) Jesus Miracle: Lazarus
"Lazarus!  Come forth!"
Like Charles Schwab, when Jesus speaks,
everyone listens.

44) The Last Supper
The menu was short:
bread for life, wine for blood
salvation for dessert.

45) The Crucifixion
Five wounds is nothing
compared to the sins that will
now be forgiven.

46) Judas
What you know about
Jesus and I wouldn't fill
a fist of nail holes.

47) The Resurrection
"Who moved the rock?"
the women asked. The figure
smiled and pointed skyward.

48) The Seven Seals
Watching the news, you'd
think all we have to do now
is wait for trumpets.

49) Doubting Thomas
If you're Jesus, then
show me your wounds, that I
might believe in you.

50) The End
You seek answers.
All Bibles promise one thing:
There is an end.  Amen.

# TEN PLACES JESUS SHED HIS BLOOD

I.
The first time Jesus shed His blood
was not in the garden.
Banged His thumb with a hammer
building bookcases before there were books.
He cursed, but that word is lost to time,
then said, *"You'll see. It won't be scrolls and papyrus forever.*
*One day I'll be in a book*
*and you're gonna need someplace to put it*
*'cause it won't be no coffee table book.*
*It won't be a conversation starter.*
*It'll be a conversation ender. Dig?*
*Hey, do you have any band aids?"*

His tool box was full of His blood.

II.
The first time He tried to bring something back
from the dead was a joke.
It bit His hand,
then scurried into the street.
Three women fainted.
A man nearly fell down the well to avoid it.
Jesus chased it for an hour
until it stopped, inexplicably,
by a fig tree sunk deep
in a tax collector's yard,
pointed at the sky,
its claw opening and curling,
then crumbled to dust.

III.
He pulled His heart out of His chest for them
like it was a secret He even had one.
Evidence.

40

They stared.
Peter licked his lips.
In his defense, they had not eaten for days.
Even after Jesus returned it to its cage
Peter would keep staring back over his shoulder
at His chest when they walked.
"Can you break it like bread and fish?" he asked.
"It isn't Mine to break," He said.
Peter would cut off a thousand ears for that heart,
even when he was full with their last supper's bread.
He would not finish the wine; what came later
he would have to stand by.
But in that other moment
(a Tuesday full of goat smells and water that tasted
like dirty coins)
he did not want to wait to eat of His flesh.
In his defense, they had not eaten for days.


IV.
Depending on what you ask,
He sweat until He bled in the garden.
Even after they ate of Him, He hungered,
His stomach spitting back the dates
and browning apple slices,
singing a hymn with the knowledge of the full.
Pass the cup.
He could fill it with just His collar sweat
and you would still know the way.
No one noticed that the apples were turning
because no one had invented electricity yet.
Back then every meal was a Carvaggio.
In any event, it was sweat, not like hard work,
but hard decisions. And fear in the knowing,
of what one will never have.
It's not a temptation if you never wanted it.

V.
He did not hang from the whipping post; He hugged it.
One soldier even said He kissed it,
but he was a raging homophobe for a Roman.

VI.
Ladies and gentlemen, fashionistas, Lenny.
Please turn your attention now to the top of the runway,
We have Jesus of Nazareth
crushingly adorned in a crown of thorns,
sporting a brim of dried leaves that is all the rage in Malta this season.
This item comes in crushed nettles and thornberry
so don't be shy: place your order now
or be damned if you don't.

VII.
This is the one He fought them over.
A man in that land is nothing without his hands.
Couldn't pull a horse, couldn't mend a neighbor's fence,
couldn't drop grapes into a wanting virgin's mouth.
Not that He was ever going to do any of those things.
But He didn't know that going in.
Somewhere along the way, nails in hands
spread like railroad timber,
He gave up those ten ghosts.

VIII.
(Insert joke about Moses & Jesus performing miracles,
to be performed as the reader sees fit.)

IX.
Dean Karnazes ran fifty marathons in fifty states in fifty
consecutive days. He's run on every continent at least twice.
When he tried to run from New York to California the first time,
he was forced to stop in St. Louis, could not forgive himself
until three years later, when he tried again and succeeded in
seventy-five days. Doctors tested him during the course of

his journey. They measured the amount of damage a human muscle sustains from exercise. They discovered that his muscles damage at a decreased rate, well below average, and that at some point they acclimate themselves to the exercise and stop being damaged altogether. It is theorized that, given sustenance along the way, he could run non-stop forever.

But he never had to run with a spear driven into his rib cage so, you know, whatever.

X.
They have called it the harrowing,
tines dragged across His name,
smoothed into metaphors for the grave
and the tomb.

A bruise at the gates of Hell.
As if life is not a hell.
As if the camel could have predicted the garage
and speaks for all garages, big and small,
or as though the prophets were very clear on the omen's tattoo.
They were not.
And because they played knuckles with God,
he bruised his son to show the world
that he was serious.

## JESUS, JUDAS, AND THE CASE OF THE OLD WOMAN'S SON
### (A Murder Mystery)

And lo I said unto Him,
"You could just raise him from the dead
and ask him who killed him."
And Jesus spoke, saying,
"Judas, you know it doesn't work that way."

We were passing through the village anyway,
following the midday star.
For days he washed feet and consoled lepers,
and I would count the money.
I wasn't greedy then, just frugal.

The old woman split her face crying for her son
and praising The Master,
brimming to her eyes with despair like love.
She offered Him twelve apples, all rotten,
passing the basket to Him humbly.
He took only the worst one, fumbled
through the fruit for it, took a bite,
and winked at me.

Jesus played dumb.
He did that a lot.
And when we were alone, He laughed.
Usually at my expense, like someone who knows
how the book ends and keeps looking over your shoulder.
He would always appear before me and ask,
"What part are you at?" and I would snap at Him
and He would kiss me on the cheek.

The old woman showed us her son.
He could not be touched. The shroud was already on him,
but we swore not to leave his side.

44

I said, "Would have been better if they kept him where he was.
We could have checked for footprints or markings."
The Master bit His apple, looked me up and down like
I was short, and spit apple chunks thusly:
"Better for the purposes of man,
but not for the purposes of the Spirit."
It was always the spirit with Him.
Just one time I'd like to turn to Him and say,
"You know...I think the SPIRIT did it!"
But then I'd have to break the bread and fish
for the next two weeks,
and He had a way of making an easy job last all day.

We washed the desert from our hands and hair,
prayed, then prayed some more.
Jesus whispered to the body, to His hands,
to the body, then back to His hands.
The wind kicked up outside,
but it was completely unrelated.
The camels brayed, tumbleweeds batting their shins.
That was not completely unrelated.

When we had finished, we went to the well
and found our man.
He was too nervous and too clean for deserts,
and, no matter how hard he tethered it,
his mule would not stand by him
in the presence of the Lord.

Jesus would not let them slay him,
and He took the man's confession looking into his eyes,
holding his cheeks in His palms
and smiling.
And the killer's tears fell to the dust in fistfuls
of passion and shame.

When we left the next day
we were already two days behind the eleven.
They would wait, but I would have to hear about it.

"Every time He is with you He is late," Peter would say.
"Go count crows," I'd say, and ignore him (as usual).

Jesus was curious,
always gripping at things to see how they worked.
We stopped by a river and He spoke thus:
"Judas,
how many loaves of bread would you lay before me
that I could not walk on this water?"
Every time He said something like this I clutched at our purse.
I knew better than to challenge The Master,
but on that day,
I gambled that He could not swim.
And as I pulled Him from the river,
choking and laughing and clutching at my neck for purchase,
He slapped my back and said thusly:
"This is why I love you, Judas:
you do not believe everything you hear.
And if anyone asks, you were baptizing Me," and shook
His hair like an animal in from the rain.

Thus sayeth the Lord,
forever and ever,
amen.

# STALAG 3:16

*"For God so loved the world, that he gave his only begotten Son, that whosoever believeth in him should not perish, but have everlasting life." —*John 3:16 KJV

For my mom so loved peace and quiet,
she gave her woebegone Son,
that whosoever believeth in keeping him
for two dusty weeks at church camp
should not perish, but have everlasting
laughter at his expense.

Two sheet metal warehouse chapels,
a wooden barn dormitory.
The *Hogan's Heroes* of church camps.

The seven o'clock baptism tub
had watermelons in it at three o'clock.
This was not coincidence.
Those slices were the sweetest communion wafer ever.
Salvation running down our chins,
their holy syrup manifested with each slurp.

Today's activity: Pray
and shut up.

*Can I call my mom?*
"Sure," a counselor told me,
then turned me around to Zanesville's hills.
"You can yell right on out here for
as long as you want. It's free, too."
As you can see, I never let go of that horrible caprice.
I wanted to kill him, knowing I could be forgiven
in a warehouse alter call shortly after.
I shouted until the hills
shrugged indifferent into darkness,

my throat raw with biblical hate and cartoon bile.
My best two-week summer friend—who would die
without a church service because he was black
and gay—carried me back to the dorm,
snuck cartons of warm chocolate milk back in the night.

Today's activity: Choose.
The ceramic Bible or the ceramic Jesus prayer hands.
Don't ponder it too long.
They only have silver paint anyway,
and given two weeks of Galilean-levels of destitution,
you'll be painting both when it's all said and done.

End-of-the-week holy ghost marathon focus groups,
as if we might brainstorm the point of spirit.
Campers panting to get saved
reciting "hallelujah" over and over
until the ghost came in sweat and tears and bitten jaws.
Speak in tongues and the watermelon's all yours.
"Hallelujah" over and over again until your tongue
sounds like you're speaking in feet.

Church camp ends like all camps end:
children who learned to love their mothers
while they were away running to the backseat
of idling cars, learning that being "saved" now has
all kinds of meanings.
The air conditioner vent in the shotgun seat
also works in mysterious ways.

Years later, at my last Vacation Bible School,
we were packed Jonestown style into the church chapel
for a mass haunting. I'd been baptized twice by then,
and I could not bring myself to lie about ghostbusting
the Holy Ghost at church camp years before;
I needed saved and I needed it right now.
But at twelve you do not hunger for vastly different things
than when you were seven.

48

I just wanted the chocolate milk,
but milk was for closers.

Fortunately I'd survived the camps.
I'd gotten all the practice I needed in Zanesville's hills,
and my hallelujahs could go on forever.
There is a part of me still chanting,
over and over, waiting
for the milk to come.

# PART III.

# THINGS I DID WHILE WRITING THIS POEM

*(With thanks to Patton Oswalt)*

My face does not know how to tell the wind
how it likes to be caressed.
The world's largest cattail
bending into the palm of the world's sigh.

> *(Things I did while writing this stanza:*
> *- Made a mixtape for an imaginary knitting party.*
> *- Read two Stephen King introductions, but none of the stories.*
> *- Stacked a pile of CDs I need to return to the library.)*

Away, autumn rings the church bell,
leaves turn Baptist,
falling into puddles below.

> *(Things I did while writing this stanza:*
> *- Changed my signature for autographs.*
> *- Read the liner notes for New Edition's* N.E. *Heartbreak.*
> *- Tried to take pictures of myself at arm's length without*
> *  showing my arm.)*

My grandmother's lantern I saved.
No need for miners' caps and canaries here.
Lights the way to the warmth of kitchens now,
coal dust and apple skin lodged in its gears.

> *(Things I did while writing this stanza:*
> *- Sang Pet UFO's "Big Flatty" into an unplugged microphone*
> *- Reordered my Netflix queue.*
> *- Killed a centipede with a receipt from Staples for staples.)*

The books lay on top of their brethren now,
no room to stand side-by-side. The ones
most likely to be read earn repose, their spines
say hello in gratitude.

*(Things I did while writing this stanza:*
- *Air dusted my turntable.*
- *Wrote an Amazon review for a book about Prince [3 stars].*
- *Tried snapping all four of my fingers in a row, failed.)*

# FLOTSAM

You find the one piece of work he left town to get.
She serves you hot meals for your trouble,
water from a well that never comes clean.

You fix the screen door that angry dust slams open and shut
like an accordion, bring another man's tool box back
to life, split the load of grime and wind.

You stop being "Mister" after twelve suppers,
become who your mother named you.
Your landlord feeds you the last can of hash she has,

finding her way to the cot you have started paying for
with sweat, fingernails rich with earth on hands like a man's
rooting your back like the ghosts of pigs that had names once.

Some evenings, easy jokes from a porch with the best view
of the dust devil crop you ever saw. Without trying,
his threadbare chair becomes yours.

The black blizzards howl outside,
sand-mouthed boarders looking for work, too,
kissing your hair, your cups, your sheets.

When you come home from the store,
your bags at the porch waiting politely,
the kitchen hot and loud with grits and sausage

she has been saving for a special occasion,
you know he's come back home. You don't even check
that your good socks are in the sack,

the spot you wore in them hitchhiking here
sewn with thread she spit on, squinted at, then thrust
through a hole no one else could see in a storm like this.

## TOPIT

Of all the tricks I know, making you disappear was the hardest.
Holding you by the hand, watching you switch across the stage,

full of peacock feathers and maps to places made of pillows,
you looked at me every time like I might actually send you away.

Like the things I do up here are real.
Even when the box went empty you remained:

a hair in the corner, a silk feather near the door,
your perfume of sweat and stage grease in my nose.

Even when you vanished for real
these familiars sat at every table with me.

Everything on the stage was a prop except our love.

When we rode the carriage into London you
turned from whispering at the river, looked me in the eye

as if I were waltzing you into a box again
and said, "Everything about a man is in his magic."

What did my bullet catch tell you, save that you would make
me risk it all? That kissing is more magic than trust?

What did snaking through a water tank reveal about our
morning afters? Did my blankets drown your dreams?

We both know why you left. It wasn't because you loved him more.
My problem was that I always showed you how the tricks were done.

You always knew where my rabbits would end up.
You knew I would kill them for the show of it.

You went to him because he never kills the rabbits.
I stopped pulling them out of hats for you. Still won't do the trick.

Everyone assumes it's because it's a base trick,
that anyone can do it. The truth is they only listened to you.

He could never show you the tricks I did,
never perform The Disappearing Man

or the Monolith or The Tank of Doom or The Wringing Bell,
never fill a room with awe or rumors of the Orient

or a cloud of flash powder.
He was parlor tricks and floating cards and doves in scarves.

He would not let you bind him in locks and chains and
drop him in a closet of sea to gauge his love.

The day I spirited my hand through a sheet of metal,
you left. You kissed me, then said the only thing you

needed to know about me you'd just seen,
that you didn't need a man who couldn't be scratched.

I've see you on the posters for his parlor shows.
Stood in the back of one once.

Saw you hold his cage and his hat and his blanket and his beasts.
One ball becomes two balls becomes three balls is not magic.

I stopped pulling rabbits from hats because they stopped
appearing at the bottom of them. Their lettuce un-eaten,

their traps as clean as answers, a colony vanished
from the savannah of your palms.

I should have sawed you in half. Then he could have his piece
and leave, your toes twiddling out the back of his suitcase.

But I would hold on to your face and your arms and your heart.
And everything I loved about you

could fill a top hat that I would wear everywhere I went
and pull rabbits from, when you let me.

# MILK

My cereal tastes like Walkman batteries,
8-track tape, 75-cent gas.
My mother is still shaking from the blizzard of '78.
My cereal tastes like light sabers.

Two blocks
made you a dairy superstar, Etan.
First time you walk to a bus stop alone
you end up on a 1979 milk carton.
You the first.
Boy trying to become a man
meets man trying to stay a boy.
My cereal tastes like bus exhaust.

Etan, we're so green now.
Milk jugs are plastic.
The cartons that remain have been scared straight
with nutritional values.
No room for a missing child's face anymore.
If we had put you on bread bags, you'd still be here.
Not HERE here, but around.
Alive in time for breakfast.
You too grim for cereal boxes,
snap crackle and kidnapped.
Your fingers and toes like prizes in the bottom.
My cereal tastes like duct tape.

Your parents never moved away.
Never know when you'll come running down the street,
wondering what happened to your old toys.
You can't fit them anymore, but all of your clothes
have come back in style.
My cereal tastes like denim.

There was a twenty-five thousand-dollar reward
for information about you.
Your mother doesn't even want her pound of flesh.
Twenty-five thousand dollars buys a lot of milk.
You got the ball rolling but there weren't enough
milk cartons in Atlanta.
Should have put their babies on the backs of menthol packs.
My cereal tastes like Atlanta.

Every year your father sends a picture of you to the only suspect.
He writes on the back of it one sentence:
"What did you do to my little boy?"
He got nothing but time,
still reads the back of every picture.
My cereal tastes like envelope paste.

It's been thirty years since you went to school.
Like you in the longest detention ever.
Thirty years, you've missed so many things.
*Jaws*, every rap song ever, remote controlled televisions, Atari.
My cereal tastes like static.

Etan, you would have passed the spelling bee that day,
but in the end you would hate writing.
Science was going to be your thing.
You would watch a sunset and tell us
it was a series of chemical reactions on a planetary scale,
the sun's gasses reflecting off of the solar panel of
the earth's atmosphere, and I'd punch you in the arm and say,
"Dude, it's a sunset.
You sit here.
You watch it.
You let it go away, without saying goodbye.
That's what beautiful things do."
My cereal tastes like sunsets.

## 24-HOUR HORROR MOVIE MARATHON

I'm not sure what my Netflix queue says about me.

The centipede of humans attached mouth to anus.

The undead woman the boys have their way with
in an abandoned hospital.

The nearly-aborted killer in search of his mother's pimp.

The virgin with an angry mouth between her thighs.

The coroner who uses obituaries like a dating service.

The French.

The woman trying to steal another woman's baby with a pair
of scissors.

The sorority girl skinned alive in search of God and
resurrection.

The only one I don't recommend to people:
The one with the most beautiful satin party dress I've ever seen
hiked up over a woman's hips in a nine-minute
real-time rape scene in a subway
boring into my mind for days.

I saw this one in a theater full of aficionados of evil,
during a 24-hour horror film marathon.
When they laughed at the decapitated priest
and the demon who lifted a baby by its ankle meat,
swallowing it whole, it was the kind of sound
that makes you worry
about the humanity of the people next to you,
the person inside of you, holding your ticket.

You fear the black-clad mob when it cheers
the up-ended roller coaster car,
showering the amusement park with body parts and hormones.

But when the most beautiful satin party dress I've ever seen
flips upward, exposing a thigh I would have killed
to see in a dark room,
splashed forty feet across my horizon,
and they are silent,
not even a popcorn husk soundtrack breaching the wall,
the only sound in nine minutes a gasp, I understood.

I leave that dark room 24 hours later,
24 hours less my life,
24 hours more my faith restored.

## I HATE ZOMBIES LIKE YOU HATE ME

Here is what I wish would happen:

A windy November day,
before the snow has spilled its milk
and the leaves still grip the ground in their stiff handshakes,
that while visiting your grandmother's gravesite,
having cleared away the autumn debris and dew dust,
I wish your grandmother would break the crust
and reach for you,
swirl her knobby, apple pie-baking bones around your ankle
and drag herself out of the trench she has been digging,
staring at you with unblinking, puss-laden eyes
yellow from a lack of sun and birthdays,
moaning from her diaphragm and her throat at once,
baring her teeth after having popped mortician stitches,
aimed at your snot-nosed five-year-old who only
wants to know if you're going to stop at
McDonald's on the way home.

I wish that in that mortifying moment you
remember how, while we sat in a theater
and the trailer for yet another zombie movie splayed across
the cinema canvas, you turned to me and said,
"Zombies are awesome."
And when I said "I am so sick of zombies,"
you tightened your lips and lost
my phone number.

I wish that your grandmother was followed
by another grandmother,
and another, and a jawless uncle who lost his way after the war.
And because it's Veterans Day, he will be a wily zombie general,
and his moans will mean something,
and on his one-armed, jawless command
every grave with a flag spits forth

63

the contents of their dingy bellies
and the zombie invasion begins,
right there, where you are,
while you try to remember
what was so cool about them in the first place.

It used to be vampires;
so fine, so literate, so thin and grazed of chin.
You used to coo over them, too, pecked at
every book featuring a woman too abundant for corsets,
two red dents of ancient love dotting her pristine neck.
Even you would have to admit that just because you've been
bitten in the neck and turned into an undead count's whore
wouldn't make you a better lover.
You would still be as ugly as you ever were.
You'd just be ugly longer.

If we are honest, we do not love the zombie.
We do not think the zombie is cool.
We do not imagine the zombie for a lover or a count or a
Tom Cruise/Brad Pitt sandwich.
None of their stories are about them.
All zombie stories are about us,
about the people who aren't zombies,
and how we scream and run and die when something
without the brain God gave a snow globe
manages to destroy us in a shopping mall.
So all zombie stories are about autumn and brains and
shopping carts and whatever else
we can throw in their shambling path
to make the un-cool undead hooligan cool again.

So here is what I wish would happen:
that *next* Veteran's Day,
when you visit the grave of your
stoic and cigar-munching grandfather,
that the wind whispers the only warning
you're apt to receive, and then?
Then you think about the fact that

64

I bought the popcorn
and the tickets
and the Gummi Bears you let fall
through the seat and shrugged at
like they didn't cost shit,
and you remember,
when Gramps is chomping at the bit from underneath you,
his Purple Heart swinging from the ventricles of his purple heart,
you remember that I was a good man
you let slip through your fingers.

## WHY YOU DON'T REMAKE *THE THING*

The original had
the greatest scientific minds in the world
battling a beast from another planet.
In the second, far superior version,
they were beer-swilling helicopter pilots.
You do not need to be a scientist to know
how to fight on this level.
Even the helicopter pilot knows fire burns.
The scientists loved it inappropriately.
The rascals? They loved it better.
This cannot be improved upon.
It can only be replayed, me lying on a couch
trying to recall our last time just as it was.
Every time I keep adding passion.
(You never smiled in that position.)
(The sun never hit you that way in that room.)
My brain is too much scientist.
My body is very much helicopter blade.

Impossibly, I found a strand of your hair
between my legs yesterday.
The Thing can replicate a person from an inch of DNA.
I want to step into the snow with your hair
and ask the monster questions,
determine how it knows what to say
when protecting itself in a foreign land,
to know if it can replicate love
and if not love, just the parts of you I want.
I would take its molecular embrace if it meant
your hips would be mine again,
forming under my palms whenever I desired.
You told me I could never sleep with a clone of you.
That was before there was a Thing
that could fix our distance.

66

Fire will destroy The Thing.
Fire will never destroy her.

In the original they had women on base,
a love story tucked into the tension of the hunt.
1984 had no such virus. Every man for himself.
No showers, no unisex restroom.
No argument about the toilet seat being up
for a thousand miles.
No love. No tears because of love. No wistfulness.
No screaming at the sink.
Just stiff pillowcases and ice and flamethrowers.
No crying until the alien comes, softening
body parts, exposing their hearts, placing men
into its womb, delivering them over and over
until the passion of gasoline like whiskey
puts her to sleep. Back to frozen manhood.
Wistful about death, but little else.

In the first they were in Alaska. The second?
Antarctica. Genius in the dunes.
The better film alienates the protagonists on a level
that a place you can drive to never could.
This cannot be improved upon.
It can only be picked at again, a scab of tone.
If you're going to be left behind, try to make it count.
Take only what you're willing to lose
and leave the rest behind. Take only music on cassettes.
Nothing else can brave the loneliness,
brave the snow you will find in everything,
like pieces of her/its hair.

You don't remake a remake, people say.
You should want me as I am: better than you know,
gleaming for you, even frozen in time.
If I can love you better, then it's worth the film.
I won't lie: we may never know who this new one is for.

# CTHULHU CALLS FOR LOVE

We are here now.
And love?
Love must be tenacious here,
where a child folds over, clutching his spilling stomach
and becomes a lightning roach,
where the widow's man sits up in his coffin
reaching for his flowers,
where the grandfathers who drowned in September
still pine for October air.

None of our binding spells keeps the bay at bay forever.
Something that walks like a man would walk
if he were shy half a leg and thirty feet tall
shambles across the skyline, tearing dusk from the sky
like ribbons from a choir girl's hair.
Fecundity is a perfume that sells
at a dollar an ounce on the dark corner.
Sometimes the tourists still find the beach
in the same place the next day.
Our steeples go unpainted from season to season,
stabbing at the sky they used to love,
and love?
Love must be tenacious here,
Past the cemetery where the stones wear their dates backwards.
The gargoyles return to their drainpipes on Fridays;
The confessionals are all larger on the inside
than they are on the outside.

But you and I?
Our masks fell from us years ago.
I have filled the belly of my mind
on the sustenance of your thoughts.
The criminal Miskatonic River laps at our feet under the dock.
We almost don't flinch at the tentacles when they pass.
We have touched the jars of the Curiosity Shoppe,

making their contents shift and wail
in their water and come out sane.
The monster under the Plankston Bridge
screams itself awake after nightmares about our love.
When I place my head to your breast
your heart whispers clearly.
Whenever I kiss you like I mean it the Old Ones stir
and we court disaster on a cosmic level, but I don't care.
And you don't care.
And Cthulhu knows the cultists don't care.
If it were up to them we'd lie in bed all day,
me sliding tongue and razor over your skin
in praise and safety, parchment not yet meant for
enchantments.  The incantations would be soft,
wisps of wonder and pink hieroglyphs
sunk into your navel and thighs, always there, always
trying to remind you of where you belong.

This entire town reeks of the call,
every house, shop and institution's brick mortared
with the blood of angels who'd lost their way and
the pulp of trees who'd had enough that chased down
men with axes one fall.

Do you remember the museum?
When we walked its halls and waved back
at the paintings that moved and shook hands with the golem?
When we tip-toed around the sarcophagus,
lost our way in the shifting garden maze for a Thursday?
When locusts served us lunch by the stone bench
because they could not chew our love from our lips?

I remember when we were children and you came for me,
when the King of Skin had his way with me in a dark place
full of light; how you cast the only spell you knew then,
how it split his lips and fingers into tentacles and how we ran.
I knew I would love you forever then.
At that shameful moment, I should have cried, should have
taken every pill in the sanitarium, but all I could think about

was your hands and tetherball poles with balls and no strings.
Every time he walks the streets now searching for new lovers,
whenever he sees you he covers his mouth and curses us,
the two baby witches from French Hill.

I was whisked away once, you remember,
and I told you I'd found my wits,
made my way back with the help of conjuring dust
and scrolls.  You could always tell
when I was hiding something from you, so I'll be honest now:
when I met the man on the other side with nails for eyes,
fish lips rent from hell hooks for a mouth and a
square hole where his guts used to be—
that you could see the hills beyond through—
he bubbled up the way out of that wretched landscape,
saying: "Love her in all ways.  Kiss her scars.
Make harp strings from the short hairs on her neck,
play them wildly every day.
And don't eat the fish on the way out; they can run here."
I came back to you, harried, mad,
covered in the soot and brimstone slime of The City,
and you wrapped me in blankets and forgiving arms,
whispering runes to me until our spirits sat still in that library,
gods among the gods.

I have felt my mouth water at funerals
consumed the toads of Innsmouth.
Someone said there's a hotel in Yuggoth now,
asked me what time it was, then set themselves
on fire near the university.
Another Tuesday.

Just being born here we are destined for Hell,
so I love you every day,
as much as a heart's spine and chambers can carry,
so that when the call comes
thick like smog and ancient algebra,
they punish me by allowing you into Heaven.
Oblivion is just a room that doesn't know it has windows.

70

You have always been there to loose the latch,
set me wild about the night,
calling your name to the red moon
and the stars that blink and whisper our names
for all eternity, like we were Old Ones
who sleep in one chamber,
worshipped by anyone who ever knew
love like this
in a place
like this.

## COMFORT WOMAN'S GOLD

1.
When she was twelve, soldiers came for her,
dragged her into the back of a grey truck.

She counted the number of blossom trees
between her home and the barracks: 87.

Everything that gave her
peace in that place, she named a god:

"You," she said to the miso soup, "are the god of bellies."
"You," she said to her sisters' backs, "are the god of warmth."
"You," she said to the cricket, "are the god of funny music."

Comfort Woman believed her gods slept
when the soldiers took her every night.

She would not believe that they had abandoned her.
She would not believe that a bayonet was better than a man.

She learned to love the smell of bleach in hospital pillows,
found salvation in a spoiled rice grain.

"You," she said to her scars, "are the god of memory."
"You," she said to the lice, "are the gods of sharing."
"You," she said to her shame, "are the god of humanity."

The tatami never became a good bed, Comfort Woman was
a princess who could feel the pea and the springs.

The day the soldiers cried, she knew the war was over.
Only the end of war could keep them from her sisters,

prostrating themselves in suicide positions in the dirt,
brimming with honor and despair.

She had seen that kind of face before.
For Comfort Woman the war would never be over.

"You," she said to their tears, "are the god of retribution."
"You," she said to the river, "are the god of baptisms."
"You," she said to the train whistle, "are the god of freedom."

2.
I saw her where I work,
trying to find the barcode on a video,

helped her without request,
traded gestures until we found our tongue.

She left the room, then returned, saying,
"Coffee break. You are so kind."

Four pieces of candy warmed my palm.
Comfort Woman does not believe in unpaid kindnesses.

Comfort Woman prayed to fifty-two different gods back then,
and still lights incense to most of them.

Some of them did not follow her to this place.
Some of them changed faces and bay at the sun.

I unwrapped a lemon drop immediately,
set it on my tongue in front of her.

She needed to know that her treasures would not end up
at back tables in staff rooms or slipped into trash cans.

She needed to know that I believe in the same gods she does.
She needed to know that cricket song sounds the same to me,
and that her treasures will never just be candy.

"You," I say to paper, "are the god of fortune."
"You," I say to pen, "are the god of chance."
"You," I say to Comfort Woman, "are the goddess of love."

## CRUISE DIRECTOR

Attention all passengers,
if I may have your attention to the front of the ship at this time.
Just a few minor details to cover before our journey.
Please be informed that shuffleboard is on the top deck,
as are the casinos and sunbathing chairs,
and that you will be given every opportunity on this journey
        to dance.

You will dance.
You will warm bellies.
You will sing songs in a heathen's tongue.
You will lie naked for months in your own waste.
You will be bitten by sea rats.

You will dance.

You will eat my rancid leftovers.
You will cook in your own sweat in the day.
You will freeze in your nakedness at night.
You will forget the feel of a spear in your hand.
You will blister where chains kiss your wrists.
You will swim in everything but water.
You will curse the darkness of a ship's belly.
You will curse the sun when it tells you a story.
You will learn to hate all stories.
You will sleep until agony becomes a lullaby.
You will gamble that death will come for you before man.
You will lose.
You will cry over unanswered prayers until you switch gods.
You will call out for Anansi and he will weave a web in the
carcasses of your children.
You will curse your orishas, wonder why your griots never saw
this one coming in the scroll of their tongues.
You will wonder where Shango's thunder has gone.

You will finally understand why Yemaya walks on water,
not because she's magical, but because the ocean is filled
to its brim with her worshippers.
You will cry when the mother whose children
are like fish can't swim when they have had their fins
clipped to one another.
You will learn to love a whip,
to kiss a shackle like a communion wafer.

You will die.
You will dance.

You will die, then I will feed you to sharks so used to my ways
        they will follow us awaiting your buffet.
You will not die, disobey me, and I will still feed you to the sharks.
You will resist until I cut, rape, stab, or shoot you into submission.

And you will dance.

So if there's anything I can do to make your enslavement
here more inhumane, please do not hesitate
to scream.

## SURVIVING A ZOMBIE APOCALYPSE

Now, you know that's not what I meant.
I'm not killing the dog
because I hate the dog,
but because he will give us away.

This has nothing to do with my slippers.

## THE RAINBOW TROUT EXTOLS HIS MANY VIRTUES TO THE SQUID

You see all that Blue?
I give you that.
We can only take it a little at a time,
but it's yours any time you want it.

You have three hearts.
I only need one, and you may keep it there,
in the mollusk of your head.
I only need know you have it.

I am only made of heart,
and your love had a hook in it once.
When I chased a dragonfly
who flew too close to the water
carrying a diamond he could not lift,
I snatched it from him for you
and then, for ten seconds, I saw it all:
gulped the Blue in killing swallows,
glared at a battleship of wood and meat,
your love the only thing to come back for

so let me place a fin on each side
of your indigestible beak when we kiss,
like you were going somewhere and I
stopped you from pushing away
sea pouring out of you in flight.

Every time you kiss me like you mean it
your tongue strips scales from my sides,
dotting your mouth with pieces of
the sky after a rainstorm. To us,
it's just a really loud neighbor
we only see in flashes, but sure,
I've seen where the colors come from.

They come from my back
and I bleed them into that Blue up there
every time you prove you love me.

Somewhere, they say,
there are people who look at our pools
like we look to the Blue,
with meaning in their hearts,
the currents making noises
when they hit the rocks
(if you can believe that).

If it's true, it's foolish.
We already know what's down here.
It's the Blue that's got all the mystery,
that keeps the secrets, that keeps on going.
This all ends at the bottom,
we can only go so far before the dust
and lagan tells us, *that's it.*
The Blue keeps us honest,
keeps the trout flying,
trying to unlock its blood and point.

My schoolmates say
we're not supposed to be together.
They call you kraken,
ask me, "How's that octopussy taste?"

I know about the shell that used to be
inside of you, the way it tried to protect
your hearts with biology,
your mantle now full of shards and legends.
Some fish cracked it out of you before me.
That was wrong, not like us at all.

I warm for your arms and your ink.
Blot me in a cloud of your black kisses.
For that? You may have my rainbow.

I can part with it if I know it's going to you,
each of us completing some biological
puzzle piece of the other until
there is only a mermaid to show for it.

# THE BOOK OF BURGERS

*To all the burgers I have loved before.*

### 1. The Billy Goat
You are why there is wind in Chicago,
your offering wafting through the streets like siren song.
The Goat: Greatest Of All Time.
I have seen the Sosa burger kill a man.
There really are no fries.
It is a meal kilned out of chupacabra meat.
You kill a tourist a day as a sacrifice to cow gods.
There isn't a Cub alive today that doesn't wish
you'd just gotten in the ballpark that day.
Belushi prayed at your altar,
his sword quartering his chest like a cross,
your menu in his throat.

### 2. Moonburger
No one believes in you.
It is no wonder one must plow through cornfields
to get to you. Like all good religions,
there is a bit of the harvest in your hymns,
the song of wheat and chopped snake
in your porch light drums.
That you give communion at a crossroads isn't ironic at all.
It's just good business.
The sin you commit every day,
the Devil must lunch with you,
folding chairs and pews ready for your sermon
of greasy mist and ground chuck.

When asked how you got this way,
Momma just says, *"Depends on what my hand grabs."*
Today she grabs a half pound of souls
that came this way before,

before there was a paint and gravel,
before there were picnic tables and signs.
The grease rolls down my lips,
wrapping my chin like a muzzle.
I can say nothing as enlightenment
washes over me.

I hear the buzz of a motorcycle tour coming,
the dust dancing in the nostrils of the cows who know what it
means.
Jesus will return today, but quietly.
He knows you will need help feeding a motorcycle tour.
He is very good with his hands,
and everyone gets a turn at the dishes.

### 3. The Heart Attack Grill
That you look like the lobby of a hospital is the cruelest caprice.
The nurses feed you with smiles
like strippers who've found their way.

Single, double, triple, quadruple bypass burgers.
Unlimited Flatliner Fries deep fried in lard.
Lucky Strikes with the plastic still on them.
Butterfat Shakes.
It is where taste on all levels goes to die.

When you walk in they weigh you,
then again when you're done.
If you have to pay when you leave
then your faith isn't strong enough.

Dr. Jon, a bedside manner just this side of a rusty guillotine,
coos and cajoles the meat into a stack Chic Young
never had enough ink or Sunday morning comic space
to shove into Dagwood's maw.

Anyplace that tells you the food is dangerous
simply must be tried.
I worship at the feet of your blank stethoscopes,
your waitresses untrained in CPR.
Adorn me in your mocking smock
so that I may engorge myself at every orifice!
My doctor is a quack! Lisinoprol fixed my blood
but gave me a cough for months! Armor my arteries
against the dust and ravages of time!
Death will take me when I agree, when I say.
Calories will become seconds, and I will time my ecstasy.
My little deaths will be covered in ketchup.

Anyone who comes for the nurses is a liar.
Blaming recurring patronage of the HAG
on the costumes of its waitresses
is like blaming masturbation on the existence of Kleenex.

RIP, Blair River, you scare us not.
600 pounds of don't-care and freedom,
the most patriotic man I have ever seen.
Where you see pneumonia I see cheeseburgers.
It is truly a taste worth dying for,
and I will show you the full measure and girth of my faith.

## 4. Nutburger
Matt's Place looks like a boat marooned by a hurricane
next to the highway, carried away from its dock,
slapped into a skeleton of factories.

But it ain't where you from, it's where you at.
Solly's in Wisconsin spent six months on a tractor
being pulled one beam at a time toward progress,
a time machine smelling of onion and butter
hobbling its way through the snow.
Your gods are where you build their altars.

The Nutburger is cooked on a skillet fired in the Jazz Age,
a cast iron heirloom. Miracle Whip and chopped nuts spread
thick over the top, an alchemy of salt, and all killing things.

**5. My Mother's Bread Burger**
is the same as your mother's bread burger:
more ball than patty, alien gray,
scoured with pepper and onion bits
sweating grease and the end of the work day.

It keeps you alive like all of the foreign objects
in a mother's cabinet keep you alive:
canned goods as old as siblings,
relish in ancient jars with missing dates.
When I cried in 1982 over
Reagan's impending nuclear dream
she laughed in my face like a whippoorwill,
opened the cabinet over the stove,
made me turn all the labels on the food out
so I'd be able to find them during a nuclear winter.

She never made a burger we didn't pray over.
You pray over all holy things.
You honor the covenant that kept you alive,
that swept away the bombs
that sent you outside swollen from grease and Kool-Aid,
praying to the setting sun
trying to catch its angels in jars
with no dates.

# SAINT VERONICA OF THE EMERGENCY ROOM

She has the kind of black eye
cartoons used to put steaks on to heal.

I pretend the erosion in my gut is a yearning,
that my express purpose for being here was to worship at her feet.
Did you hear that, Saint Veronica? Someone loves you still.

One day? People are going to leave scratched wedding bands
on your doorstep, make a shrine under the image of Jesus
made by your blood in a tissue left on an emergency room floor.

Someone will hammer a statue of you out of purple meat,
smooth the marbled veins soft where your right eye closed
for breakfast every Saturday.

We will spend five days around your birthday in a parade
of swollen masks, broken feathers, cracked limbs,
throw blood clots into the crowd.

Someday people are going to pray to you on Sunday afternoons
before football games end, and they will weep at either outcome.

A time will come when the utterance of your name will mean
"takes a good punch and smiles."
The time is coming soon because you are here, with me, now,
Monday morning,

but today? Today, when your name is called
in this antiseptic cathedral it'll be
just like when you were in school.

And just like then, you won't care what anyone thinks
when you walk by, and you still won't know
what the extra milk carton that keeps appearing
next to your lunch tray is for.

# MISTAKEN

What I say about you
I say about myself, but don't believe.
I say you are morning.
Only night rests in my jowls.
I say you are where poetry needs to go,
even though I know it's already there.

I could taste the ruins in your mouth,
where the men who planted flags on your breasts
discovered the person already living there
and declared her "found."
The brick clay mission they made you build
in your belly is patched and crumbling,
yet your eyes still worship there,
still break wafers over their plates,
staring back into the distant past.
Feed me the cracker of your body
and wonder why I still hunger.

This is why your kisses tasted like
the book I didn't realize I'd read until it was over,
the song I have remembered all wrong,
danced to all wrong,
filled the bar we talked in with too much smoke and light.

So I say you are a construct.
I say you are not the chicken wings and
the sausage and peppers or the pillow of your hair.
You are not the knot in the kerchief of Baldwin's throat,
or the gravel piling up in your scars.
I have written so many odes to your scars
you have been rubbed smooth with tongue.

These things look back in a mirror at me
every morning you are not here.

The morning you never stayed to savor,
the here that you were never in,
the you that you never were.

# I REMEMBER ME

I remembered today that I'd forgotten
that I made love to you.

I would offer that you not take this as a slight.
I did, after all, remember.

I even remember your name. Not everyone can say that.
I'd provide you with eyewitness proof,
but I don't know where they are now.

I even remember where: that house you rented?
On that one street? I don't remember the street.
But I remember you!

I even remember your sounds.
I have always had an ear for sounds.

I will never remember what song was playing,
but I can guarantee you that there was one playing.

I still have that...no I don't.
That was someone else. Sorry.

I am starting to wonder if you remember me,
if you can recall those horrible Berber burns you got.

I don't mean remember every day.
I mean at all.

I remembered today that I'd forgotten
that I made love to you.

I made love to you.
You may have very well made love to me back.

I don't remember.

## BLURBS FOR POETRY BOOKS I DIDN'T LIKE

This book is filled with passion. The poet's love for their own work is evident.

One can only imagine the hours he must spend reciting his work to himself.

Not what I expected at all.

This poet's work has energy.

This book is not without its merits.

Something tells me this collection will find its audience with no trouble at all.

I am speechless.

Stunning.

This writer is prolific in a way that suggests a singular dedication to their muse, who must be very tired by this point.

There is something to be said for having waited this long to compile one's book of poetry: it has given the audience time to breathe and the work time to mature.

The work reminds us of the banality of everyday problems, and the pain associated with encountering them over and over on and off the page.

The Art lies in hiding the art, Horace tells us, and this poet has literally buried the Art.

Yeats said poetry arises from the quarrel we have with ourselves, to which we are left to surmise that the work presented here is a testimony to a knock-down, drag-out furniture-ripping debate over the poet's self-worth.

With their characteristic virtues intact, the artist here seeks to name the un-nameable, put to word that which never had a word put to it before.

This poetry is the poetry of experience, and recalls the lone septuagenarian who refused to kick the can at the end of the Twilight Zone episode in which life, in its symbolic way, has passed him by and he searches, ever more deeply, into himself.

The poet stands naked here, and one cannot help but stare— mouth open, jaw dropped, belly churning with chaotic awe-at the display presented before us.

The formality of this collection is so discrete as to have no formality whatsoever.

Work that deserves to be read by others.

# THE SUNOCO STATION

Okay, now?
I'm going to need you to focus,
to listen.
Don't get hung up on the fact
that I just stepped out of a time machine shaped like
the toy chest in our mom's basement.

Go ahead: kiss Raynelle behind her grandmother's garage.
Even though she is not the one for you,
you will cherish it forever.
You have already forgotten about the molesters.
This is as it should be.
You have legs made of Big Wheel tires
that can walk without those crutches.
Do not let William Rogers borrow your nunchakus. You will
lose a tooth.
Do not tell Melissa Anderson you love her on the school bus.
You will mean it, but you have no idea what she is capable of.

Listen:

Keep every toy you have.
Start writing down the titles of every book you're going to read.
Get into the blues now before you realize
why you'll need them later.
Do not trade your Metal Men comic books for
White Boy Kevin's spare Atari controller. It's broken.

Listen:

Do not feel guilty about the Sunoco station.
That wasn't your fault.
They were going to beat you up anyway.

It's no coincidence that once you took a swing they left.
Even though you missed and your fist
was practically an apology fast becoming a caress,
it was the thought that counted.
When it comes to bullies, you really do get extra credit for trying.

Every one of them will get what's coming to them,
even the one who stood in the back making sour patch faces.
I checked.
One of them I even made sure of myself,
the one with scars for tears?
He was doomed the minute he made you pay
for the crimes of his father with his knuckles,
every finger ten times a hundred times
our mother loved us back.
Even now I am churning him,
immortalizing his weaknesses.
He will have to carbon date any good in his life
to the day before you met and I have
gone out of my way to make it look like
evolution is a devil's prank.

Listen:

Don't start up with that girl in tenth grade.
She's going to die young and you will not weather it.
Don't feed the goldfish so much.
Don't let your brother talk you into that grass-cutting job.
You are going to be awesome when you learn when to shut up.
Know that when you have a pen in your hand God is speaking.

Listen:

I know what you want to do.
You want to learn how to fight back.
I can tell you from experience that's mine that's yours to be,
you will fail.
The bullets you borrow will never hit their marks,

the knives, while impressive, will never go where you meant
them to.

Don't steal the key to the Spanish test.
Don't try to turn every three friends you make into a
movement.
Stick with painting.
Stop writing poems for Michelle Norwood.  She is so
uninterested.
You will lose three children.
One of them you will be unable to do anything about
except write poems.
They will never hear them.
Right now, that won't mean much.
You still haven't learned regret.

You will punch holes in your spirit like a drunken god
trying to make up for the Sunoco station.
It wasn't your fault.
I know. I was there.
And I'm sorry that I could only stand
in the back and watch you learn
how to become a man.

# THE SLAVE WRITES OF WAGON WHEELS

Of all the plantations I have had the
displeasure to attend, I've found none
more dissatisfying than this one.

Take these slave quarters. Look at this mess.
Is that pile of hay supposed to be a bed?
Didn't think I'd have to mint my own pillows.
I wouldn't let Massa's horse eat off this floor.

We stand now in a plantation comprised
of such awe-inspiring squalor that
one is forced to laud Satan for his
abominable decorating skills.
How is one to venture forth in public
to pick cotton in sackcloth such as this?

It should go without saying that the food?
A terrific comedy of errors.
The cornmeal is rank, the catfish gamey,
and the pork was cooked over a candle
within an inch of its many maggots.
The biscuits, while cold, were serviceable,
which is what one has come to expect from
a side dish meant to serve a family
of five working a field the live-long day.

There isn't enough meat in this slop to
build a housefly. I'd rather have my tongue
driven under a stone wagon wheel, then
corkscrewed into whip twine than dine here again.

The grease that has been left behind for the
hair care needs of long-term guests comes from the
back axle of an 1864
Surrey two-seater wagon, which any

Tom will tell you is like cutting corners
on a worn pair of hand-me-down slave boots.

I can offer this bit of northern light
at the bottom of the drinking gourd: a
finer collection of whips you'll not find.

And while I have often been lambasted
for a palette that suggests my ego
be driven hot from my back in lashes,
for having a tongue full of presumption
where spit and anger should be, rest assured:

I know.

I do not seek out these reviews so much
as, like Manifest Destiny, they are
occasions thrust upon my person.
God forbid, left to my own devices
in Africa that I might cure cancer.

Take it from me: minstrels pretending to
the throne of antebellum savoir-fare
will attempt to sell you a bill of goods
shaped like stump speech you have long since timbered.
From me, you receive only the finest
elocution a self-made, illegal
education has to offer. I know
my place, and it will be at the front of
history.